SUMMARY

OF

WIN: ACHIEVE PEAK ATHLETIC PERFORMANCE, OPTIMIZE RECOVERY AND BECOME A CHAMPION.

BY DR. JAMES DINICOLANTONIO

D1733377

ANDY C. HICKERMAN

Aside feeling insecure and unconfident about yourself as a result of excessive weight, excess weight is a major contributor to many sicknesses and even death in extreme cases. Cases abound where overweight people go all out to find solutions to their weight problem and sometimes end up doing the wrong thing which might adversely affect their bodies.

In the book titled "WIN", authors; Dr. James Dinicolantonio, Siim Land,

Tristein Kennedy proffer in noncomplex terms, the secrets to perfect physical development and fitness. Through this book, they teach and highlight the major ways through which an individual could develop their bones and muscles, shed excess fats in the body as well as become as physically fit as possible. The book also reveals the right food and meal plan to go with whenever one decides to embark on the journey of physical development and fitness. The book is most suitable for athletes, body builders as well as other individuals who are interested in maintaining a healthy, fit and developed body

Improving athletic performance is easier than before with the latest innovations in technology and training methodologies Athletes today now perform various things which people thought was impossible. But where does one start as a beginner if he wants to improve his athletic performance? The Authors in this book answers this question as well as the right guideline to follow in order to achieve this goal.

Athletic performance can be seen as the effort that an athlete makes to achieve a particular performance goal over a specific time period. Athletes' natural talent and fitness influences their level of performance. Ultimately, all athletes measure their performances on their own standards. Athletes' performance is influenced by five factors: body proportions, skill training, strength, flexibility and endurance. Body proportions determines the mass of an individual. This has a significant impact on a person's overall performance in exercise. The training one gets determines how well they perform in a given exercise. Getting the perfect training and workouts, develops the individual's body as well as his mind towards his set goals. Athletics consists of ten major components that make up what we call complete athletics or balanced fitness. These components see the full functioning of an athlete in his everyday activity.

Weight loss can result from loss of fluid, muscle mass, or fat. Fluid loss can be caused by medication, water loss, lack of water intake, or illnesses such as diabetes. Loss of body fat can be deliberately brought about by exercise or dieting, for example, if you are overweight or obese. There are health benefits attached with reduction of weights. These include lowering cholesterol and blood sugar, lowering blood pressure, reducing stress on bones and joints, and reducing work on the heart. Maintaining weight loss is important for lifelong health benefits. There are essential advantages associated with weight loss program which an individual ought to know. These benefits keep one motivated during his difficult moment and prevent the individual from slacking.

Every journey to lose weight comes to a difficult point. To be successful, you need to consider all the different ways you can improve your social life, physical and mental health by losing weight. Individuals at this point ought to put down the benefits of weight loss which they want to achieve in their weight loss journey. Visit the list on a disappointing day and remind yourself the reason you embarked on this journey. You do not have to lose your excess fats at once before you start seeing result in your body and health. If you are currently overweight or obese, you may lose very little weight to improve your overall health. In addition to health benefits, you can also experience lifestyle improvements by losing weight. Those who succeed in losing weight report improved sleep, reduced stress, improved self-confidence, improved body image, improved energy, improved mood, improved sex life, and improved vital health benefits.

According to a 2019 scientific review, exercise is as effective as other first-line treatments in the treatment of depression and is rarely used as a treatment. Another 2013 article in the Frontier Magazine of Psychiatry looked at the relationship between physical activity and anxiety. Researchers have found that extra exercise enhances self-efficacy and enhances the ability of those who are confident in their success. Excursing your body on a regular basis is very imperative to the body. It acts as a distraction to anxiety. It does this by lowering these anxiety symptoms and then helps you focus on a particular goal or objective. Some individuals who are in a relationship, most of the times lose weight just to please their partners and save their relationships. It should be noted that this reason for losing weight is not ideal as you are doing so to please another person and not for your own benefits. Most times, this goal of losing weight backfires when they are faced with another problem and hence end of gaining those weight they initially lost. Dieting and exercising to make others happy can help you lose weight at first, but most individuals often return to their initial body mass. Social support can certainly have a positive effect on your weight loss journey, but to ensure long-term success, you have to set goals for yourself and stick on those goals.

There are lot of benefits derived from developing thin muscles in an individual. Increase bone density, controlled weight to a great extent reduce the risk of chronic illness, and improve quality of life. Muscles act as motors that burn calories even when you are resting. In fact, calories are burned faster when one develops muscles. As the old saying goes," use or lose it. when we do not use the muscles, it diminishes as the day goes by. It is advisable that one engages in exercise that will not only develop their muscles but keep them in an appropriate shape and mass relative to their whole body mass. Exercise like planking helps in the development of the muscles. However, it is important to remember that health is more important than the numbers on the scale.

Ideally, weight loss means losing fat while gaining muscle mass at the same time. There are some diets that fastens the process of weight loss. However, this can cause the body to burn muscle after burning a certain amount of fat. And muscle destruction slows down the body's metabolism.

Diet and exercise are closely related to losing weight. The

two go hand in hand. When you exercise to develop our muscle, you should also supplement it with the right diet, if not the entire process amounts to nothing. The right food should also be taken at the right time and at the right quantity. Food rich in protein, calcium and minerals should be taken regularly. The American College of Sports Medicine discovered that "about 10% of muscles are lost by the age of 50," and muscles continue to atrophy even after that. This issue is frequent in women than in men due to the fact that they lack the hormone required for proper muscle development and maintenance. Still, strength training is important at any age. Weightlifting, squats and push-ups are just a few examples. While engaging in these muscle development exercise, ensures that you have adequate rest and sleep as they are imperative to a proper muscle development

Dietary planning helps ensure that you eat a wide variety of foods, helps you eat more fruits and vegetables, and helps reduce your risk of chronic diseases that affects the body and inhibits its function. Following a healthy diet will also help ensure that you are consuming the right foods with the right servings. Eating more genuine foods reduces the intake of highly processed foods that are low in calories but rich in calcium. Eating more genuine foods reduces your intake of processed foods and reduces your risk of obesity

The immune system plays an important role: it protects your body from pollutants, bacteria, and cellular changes that can make you sick. It is composed of various organs, cells and proteins. As long as your immune system is functioning properly, you won't even notice it is there. White blood cells are a major facilitator in your immune system. They are produced in your bone marrow and are part of the lymphatic system. White blood cells gets to different parts of the body system by moving through the blood and tissues, looking for foreign invaders (microorganisms) such as bacteria, viruses, parasites, and fungi. As we age, our immune system deteriorate. They are no longer stronger like they were during our childhood. The Authors through this book reveals why It is imperative at this point that we take measures and ensure that we avoid the wrong kind of foods that further affects our immune system as well as incorporate the right lifestyle that improves or maintains the immune system, the meals to eat and the exercises to incorporate in our daily routine.

The quest for a healthy and fit lifestyle cannot be overemphasized. Individuals have always sought the need to attain the best when it comes to body fitness as well as body development. This book gives us an in-depth knowledge on physical development and fitness of the body. It does not only explain the need for physical development but also the way to achieve this supported by scientific evidence. It is an ideal book for all individuals on the journey of physical development and body fitness.

Manufactured by Amazon.ca
Bolton, ON

24689475R00015